30 minute Indian meals made simple

Exclusive to Howdens Joinery Co.

HOWDENS

JOINERY CO.

MAKING SPACE MORE VALUABLE

Sunil Vijayakar

30 minute Indian meals made simple

We're all busy people these days, so any ideas for preparing tasty meals quickly are very handy. Fortunately, this book is full of them!

With Indian cooking, there are many shortcuts to packing in the flavour. Simply by using the right combinations of spices and herbs, you can create wonderfully complex-tasting dishes in minutes. And that's what these recipes are about: getting the right ingredients (all widely available) and turning them into something truly irresistible in just a few easy steps.

You can have any of them ready within 30 minutes – and many much faster. Whether you're preparing a midweek family meal, a relaxed lunch for friends or a lavish dinner party, you'll spend less time cooking and more time enjoying the dishes you've made.

All the recipes have been tested using Lamona appliances, so you can be confident they'll turn out well. Whether you're a keen cook or just starting to try your hand in the kitchen, you'll find it easy to achieve those authentic Indian flavours and aromas.

The Lamona range is all about choice and versatility – and with these recipes, you'll have many opportunities to discover all the great features of our products.

Sunil Vijayakar

Food Stylist and Author

The Indian Kitchen

For Indian families, the kitchen is definitely the heart of the home; a place not only for cooking, but also for eating, entertaining and socialising. It's a big part of everyday life and culture, so the room's design is strongly influenced by the country's rich colours and textures, and exotic architecture. On a practical level, plenty of storage space is essential. With a wealth of ingredients in many recipes – especially all the herbs and spices – you'll always find well-organised shelves and drawers.

Our Indian Connection

Since Howdens started in 1995, curry has become part of our culture too.

Although our business is a national one, it runs very much on a local level, where decisions are made in each of our 565 depots based on local knowledge and customer needs.

So getting Howdens people together regionally to discuss the issues of the day over a curry has become a regular and important way of airing views and sharing thoughts.

This tradition has become such a part of Howdens life that every year we give an award to the 'Best Indian Restaurant in the UK', nominated by each region, and judged by one of Howdens' directors.

Because of our great love of curry, it seemed highly appropriate that the theme of this cookbook should be Indian food – featuring dishes you can cook at home in your own Howdens kitchen, using Lamona appliances.

We invited respected food stylist and author Sunil Vijayakar to create our book of 47 recipes, which are simple to prepare in 30 minutes or less. All of Sunil's dishes pictured were cooked using Lamona appliances.

Our Journey Continues

Our depot managers know a good curry when they taste one. Here's a
selection of the Indian restaurants they've enjoyed over the years – we
hope you like them too.

The Cinnamon Tree
Tonteg Road, Treforest,
Pontypridd, Wales, CF37 5UA.

Saffron
Axis 4-5 Woodlands Business Park, Woodlands,
Bradley Stoke, Bristol, BS32 4JT.

Spice Guru
27 Bell Street, Reigate, Surrey, RH2 7AD.

Star of India
5 Abington Avenue, Northampton, NN1 4NY.

Mr Singh's
India Gate, Perth Road, Dunblane, FK15 0EY.

Calcutta Club
London Road, Polhill, Halstead, Kent, TN14 7AA.

The 3 Singh's
254 Sticker Lane, Bradford, BD4 8RN.

Double Tree
323 Garstang Road, Fulwood, Preston, PR2 9UP.

If you appreciate good Indian food, here are some of Sunil's favourite
restaurants around the country.

Gymkhana
42 Albemarle Street, London, W1S 4JH.

The Chilli Pickle
17 Jubilee Street, Brighton, BN1 1GE.

The Viceroy
8-9 Midland Road, Derby, DE1 2SN.

rters

ndian meal can begin in many different ways —
 with something quite substantial. These starters
st as interesting and tasty as the main courses,
include three very different kinds of kebabs,
stible seafood cakes, spiced yogurt soup and,
urse, crispy onion bhajis.

Paneer Tikka Kebabs

Paneer Tikka Kebabs

Paneer is a fresh-tasting cheese, commonly used in Indian cookery. With a light flavour and dense, crumbly texture, it pairs beautifully with strong, spicy flavours. Try these kebabs with a fresh kachumber salad and warmed chapatis or naan bread.

Serves 4 10 mins preparation, 10-12 mins cooking

Ingredients
400g paneer cheese, diced
2 tablespoons ready-made tikka masala paste
200g whole milk natural yogurt
Juice of 1 lime
2 tablespoons fresh coriander leaves,
finely chopped
2 tablespoons fresh mint leaves, finely chopped
Sea salt and milled black pepper
1 red pepper, deseeded and cut into
bite-sized pieces
1 yellow pepper, deseeded and cut into
bite-sized pieces

To serve
Lime wedges
Kachumber (see page 80 for my recipe)
Chapatis or naan bread

8 metal skewers

1. In a bowl, mix together the tikka masala paste, yogurt, lime juice and a tablespoon each of the chopped coriander and mint. Season well with salt and pepper. Add the paneer and mix well to coat evenly.

2. Thread the paneer cubes onto 8 metal skewers, alternating them with the pepper pieces.

3. Place the kebabs on a lightly oiled grill rack and put under a pre-heated medium-hot grill for 10-12 minutes, turning once and basting with any remaining tikka mixture. The paneer and peppers should be lightly charred at the edges.

4. Arrange the kebabs on a serving platter, and sprinkle with the remaining chopped coriander and mint. Serve immediately with lime wedges to squeeze over, accompanied by kachumber and warmed chapatis or naan bread.

Onion Bhajis

Onion Bhajis

You can see these crispy, spicy fritters all over India – especially at roadside stalls. They're hugely popular here too, and this homemade version is well worth a little effort. I love them with my coriander and coconut chutney.

Serves 4 6-8 mins preparation, 20 mins cooking

Ingredients
2 medium onions, halved and thinly sliced
200g chickpea flour (often called gram flour)
1 teaspoon coriander seeds, crushed
2 teaspoons cumin seeds
1 teaspoon hot chilli powder, and extra
to sprinkle
1 teaspoon mild curry powder
½ teaspoon ground turmeric
Juice of ½ lemon
Sea salt
150-200ml water
Vegetable oil for deep frying

To serve
Coriander and coconut chutney
(see page 80 for my recipe)

1. Place the onions in a bowl with the chickpea flour, coriander seeds, cumin seeds, chilli powder, curry powder, turmeric and lemon juice. Season well with salt and gradually add 150-200ml water, stirring until the onions are thoroughly coated in a thick, spicy batter.

2. Half fill a saucepan with vegetable oil. Place over a high heat, until it reaches 180°C (or until a cube of bread browns in 20-25 seconds).

3. Working in batches, spoon heaped tablespoons of the mixture into the hot oil and cook for 3-4 minutes, turning once, until lightly browned and crispy. Remove from oil and place on kitchen paper to drain.

4. If you like extra spice, sprinkle with a little chilli powder. Serve with the coriander and coconut chutney.

Tandoori Prawn and Mango Kebabs

Tandoori Prawn and Mango Kebabs

Juicy, spiced prawns and sweet chunks of mango go together perfectly for a quick, easy and delicious starter.

Serves 4 6-8 mins preparation, 6-8 mins cooking

Ingredients
1 teaspoon garlic paste
1 teaspoon ginger paste
1 tablespoon ready-made tandoori paste
100g whole milk natural yogurt
1 teaspoon runny honey
2 tablespoons vegetable oil
Juice of 1 lemon
24 raw tiger or king prawns, peeled and with the veins removed (leave the tails on if you prefer)
400g mango flesh, cut into bite-sized pieces
Sea salt

To serve
Lime wedges
2 tablespoons fresh coriander leaves, finely chopped
1 mild fresh red chilli, deseeded and finely chopped

8 metal skewers

1. In a large bowl, mix together the garlic paste, ginger paste, tandoori paste, yogurt, honey, vegetable oil and lemon juice.

2. Stir in the prawns and mango cubes, season with salt and mix well.

3. Thread the prawn and mango pieces alternately onto 8 metal skewers.

4. Place the kebabs on a lightly oiled grill rack and put under a pre-heated medium-hot grill for 6-8 minutes, turning once. Cook until the prawns are pink throughout.

5. Serve immediately with lime wedges, garnished with chopped coriander and red chilli.

Coriander Chicken Kebabs

To keep things simple when you're entertaining, you can prepare these appetising chicken skewers up to a day in advance. When you're ready to cook them, just pop them under the grill.

Serves 4 10 mins preparation, 10-12 mins cooking

Ingredients

6 skinless, boneless chicken breasts, each cut into 4 long strips
1 teaspoon garlic paste
1 teaspoon ginger paste
1 fresh red chilli, roughly chopped
4 tablespoons coconut cream
2 tablespoons whole milk natural yogurt
1 teaspoon ground cumin
½ teaspoon ground turmeric
1 tablespoon ground coriander

Juice of 1 lime
50g fresh coriander (stalks and leaves), roughly chopped
1 small handful fresh mint leaves, roughly chopped
2 tablespoons vegetable oil
Sea salt and milled black pepper

Food processor
8 metal skewers

1. In a food processor, add the garlic paste, ginger paste, chilli, coconut cream, yogurt, cumin, turmeric, ground coriander, lime juice, fresh coriander and mint leaves. Pour in the oil, season well with salt and pepper, and blend until fairly smooth.

2. Place the chicken strips in a mixing bowl and spoon the mixture over the chicken, coating evenly. You can then keep the chicken in the fridge for up to 24 hours.

3. When you're ready to cook the kebabs, thread the chicken onto 8 metal skewers and place on a lightly oiled grill rack. Cook under a medium-hot grill for 10-12 minutes, turning halfway, until cooked through and tender.

4. Serve immediately.

Coriander Chicken Kebabs

Machi Masala Vadas

Machi Masala Vadas

Perfect as canapés or a starter, these spicy fish cakes are packed with the punchy, fresh flavours of garlic, ginger, coconut, chilli, coriander and mint. To save time when you're entertaining, you can prepare the mixture up to a day in advance and chill in the fridge until you're ready to cook.

Serves 4 10-15 mins preparation, 12-15 mins cooking

Ingredients

200g skinless, boneless salmon fillet, roughly chopped
200g skinless, boneless cod fillet, roughly chopped
300g raw tiger prawns, roughly chopped
1 fresh red chilli, deseeded and finely chopped
1 large handful fresh coriander leaves, chopped
1 large handful fresh mint leaves, chopped
1 teaspoon coconut cream
2 teaspoons garlic paste
1 teaspoon ginger paste
1 tablespoon mild or medium curry powder

100g fresh white breadcrumbs
1 small egg, beaten
Sea salt and milled black pepper
Vegetable oil for brushing

To serve
Lime wedges

Food processor

1. Place all of the ingredients (except the oil and a small amount of coriander to garnish) in a food processor, seasoning well with salt and pepper. Blend until everything is well mixed and fairly smooth.

2. Pre-heat the oven to 220°C/fan 180°C/gas mark 6.

3. With wet hands, divide the mixture into 20 portions and shape each one into a flat cake.

4. Line a baking sheet with non-stick baking paper, and place the cakes onto it in a single layer. Brush each one lightly with a little vegetable oil, and bake in the oven for 12-15 minutes, or until slightly puffed up and lightly golden.

5. Serve warm or at room temperature, garnish with coriander and lime wedges on the side to squeeze over.

Akuri

As well as being a scrumptious starter, this quick Parsi spiced egg dish is perfect for a relaxed Sunday brunch. For a richer, creamier version, use four ducks eggs instead of the six regular eggs.

Serves 4   10 mins preparation, 10 mins cooking

Ingredients
2 tablespoons butter
1 red onion, finely diced
2 large garlic cloves, finely chopped
1 teaspoon ginger, grated
1 fresh red chilli, deseeded and finely sliced
2 teaspoons cumin seeds
1 large tomato, deseeded and finely chopped
1 handful fresh coriander leaves, finely chopped
6 large eggs, lightly beaten
100ml single cream or crème fraîche
Sea salt

To serve
Warm buttered toast

1. Melt the butter in a large non-stick frying pan over a medium heat, and fry the onion for about 5 minutes, or until soft but not coloured.

2. Add the garlic, ginger, chilli and cumin seeds, and fry for a further minute.

3. Add half the tomato and half the coriander. Stir and cook gently for another minute.

4. Whisk the eggs with the single cream or crème fraîche, and season well with salt.

5. Take the pan off the heat, and pour in the egg mixture. Return the pan to a medium-low heat, and stir with a wooden spoon until the mixture is slightly set – it should have a creamy texture and will take about 6-8 minutes.

6. Quickly stir in the remaining tomato and coriander.

7. Serve immediately over slices of freshly buttered toast.

Kadhi

Kadhi

Kadhi is a traditional Gujarati dish – a wonderful sweet, sour and spicy yogurt soup, thickened with chickpea flour. This is the classic recipe, which you can enhance by adding other vegetables. Try it with flat breads or rice, and be careful not to boil over a high heat, as it tends to curdle.

Serves 4 10 mins preparation, 20 mins cooking

Ingredients

1 litre water
500ml whole milk natural yogurt
4 tablespoons chickpea flour
(often called gram flour)
4 fresh green chillies, slit lengthways
1 tablespoon ginger paste
1 tablespoon jaggery or palm sugar
1 teaspoon ground turmeric
1 teaspoon sea salt

2 tablespoons vegetable oil
2 dried red chillies, broken into pieces
8 fresh curry leaves
1 teaspoon cumin seeds
1 teaspoon black mustard seeds
1 pinch asafoetida powder (optional)
1 handful fresh coriander leaves,
roughly chopped

1. In a large saucepan, mix the water, yogurt and chickpea flour until smooth.

2. Add the green chillies, ginger paste, jaggery or palm sugar, turmeric and salt.

3. Bring the mixture to the boil, and then immediately reduce the heat to low and cook for about 8-10 minutes, stirring regularly.

4. Heat the oil in a small frying pan over a medium heat, and stir-fry the dried red chillies, curry leaves, cumin seeds, mustard seeds and asafoetida powder (if you're using it) for 2-3 minutes, or until the seeds start to pop.

5. Stir this spiced oil mixture into the saucepan and scatter with coriander.

6. Serve hot, ladled into warmed, shallow bowls.

Meat & Poultry

These recipes cover the length and breadth of Indian cuisine, and show how it's possible to transform meat and poultry into so much more than a typical curry. Most importantly, they're very easy to make – and you can have them on the table in no time!

Chettinad Chicken Curry

Chettinad is a region of the Southern Indian state of Tamil Nadu, which is well known for its cuisine – and some very grand temples. The food tends to be on the hot and spicy side, so this dish is not for the faint-hearted! If you prefer a milder curry, reduce the quantities of black pepper and chilli powder to suit your taste.

Serves 4 10 mins preparation, 20 mins cooking

Ingredients
4 tablespoons vegetable oil
1 teaspoon black mustard seeds
8-10 fresh curry leaves
2 teaspoons ground cumin
1 teaspoon ground coriander
1 teaspoon ground turmeric
2 teaspoons sea salt
2 tablespoons milled black pepper
3 teaspoons chilli powder
800g skinless, boneless chicken thighs
or breasts, thinly sliced
400ml coconut milk

1 teaspoon ginger paste
100ml water
Juice of 1 lime

To serve
1 small handful of fresh coriander leaves, chopped (optional)
Basmati rice

1. Heat the oil in a non-stick saucepan over a medium heat. Add the mustard seeds, and when they start to pop, add the curry leaves and stir-fry for 30 seconds.

2. Add the cumin, coriander, turmeric, salt, pepper and chilli powder, and stir-fry for 1-2 minutes. Add the chicken and stir-fry for another 1-2 minutes.

3. Stir in the coconut milk, ginger paste and water. Mix well and bring to the boil.

4. Reduce to a medium heat and cook for 12-15 minutes, making sure the chicken is cooked through.

5. Remove from the heat, stir in the lime juice and garnish with chopped coriander, if you're using it.

6. Serve with basmati rice.

Chettinad Chicken Curry

Bombay Green Chicken Masala

Bombay Green Chicken Masala

If you're looking for a different way to make chicken curry, this recipe is very easy, yet full of spicy flavours. Chicken breasts are used here, but skinless, boneless chicken thighs work just as well.

Serves 4 6-8 mins preparation, 20 mins cooking

Ingredients
3 tablespoons vegetable oil
1 cinnamon stick
1 teaspoon whole coriander seeds, crushed
2 teaspoons cumin seeds
10 black peppercorns
3-4 green cardamom pods, bruised
7-8 cloves
6 skinless, boneless chicken breasts, cut into bite-sized pieces (or 700g skinless, boneless chicken thighs)
Sea salt

1 fresh green chilli
2 teaspoons ground cumin
½ teaspoon ground turmeric
2 teaspoons garlic paste
1 teaspoon ginger paste
400g whole milk natural yogurt

To serve
Basmati rice
Poppadoms

Food processor

For the green masala paste
100g fresh coriander (stalks and leaves), roughly chopped
20g fresh mint leaves, chopped

1. To make the green masala paste place all the paste ingredients in a food processor and blend until fairly smooth.

2. Heat the oil in a large, non-stick frying pan over a medium heat and add the cinnamon stick, coriander seeds, cumin seeds, peppercorns, cardamom pods and cloves. Stir-fry for 30 seconds, then add the green masala paste.

3. Stir-fry for a further 1-2 minutes, then stir in the chicken.

4. Stir fry for 1-2 minutes more, turn the heat to medium-low and cover the pan. Cook for another 15 minutes, stirring occasionally, making sure the chicken is cooked through.

5. Remove from the heat, season with salt and serve with basmati rice and poppadoms.

Kheema Mutter

This is Indian comfort food: a simple, rustic dish of minced lamb and peas, cooked with warming spices. For a filling supper, serve with any Indian bread or rice.

Serves 4 6-8 mins preparation, 20 mins cooking

Ingredients
1 tablespoon vegetable oil
200g onion, chopped
700g minced lamb
2 teaspoons garlic paste
2 teaspoons ginger paste
2 tablespoons mild or medium curry paste
6 tablespoons tomato purée
1 cinnamon stick
500ml chicken, beef or vegetable stock
500g carton passata with onion and garlic

2 tablespoons tomato ketchup
200g frozen peas

To serve
Basmati rice
Raita
1 small handful fresh coriander leaves, chopped

1. Heat the oil in a saucepan. Add the onion and mince, and stir-fry over a high heat for 2-3 minutes, until the mince is browned.

2. Add the garlic paste, ginger paste and curry paste, and cook for a further minute.

3. Add the tomato purée, cinnamon stick, stock, passata and ketchup, and mix well.

4. Bring to the boil and cook over a medium-high heat for 10-12 minutes, stirring often.

5. Add the peas, bring back to the boil and cook for 3-4 minutes, or until the peas are tender.

6. Serve with basmati rice and raita, and garnish with chopped coriander.

Kheema Mutter

Seekh Kebabs

Seekh Kebabs

For a satisfying main meal, try these succulent kebabs with flatbreads, and a cooling raita like my cucumber, mint and pomegranate recipe. You can use any minced meat, but I think lamb or beef works best with the mint.

Serves 4 6-8 mins preparation, 12 mins cooking

Ingredients

500g minced lamb or beef
Sea salt and milled black pepper
1 small onion, very finely chopped
2 tablespoons garlic paste
2 teaspoons ginger paste
1 teaspoon chilli paste
½ teaspoon ground cardamom seeds
2 teaspoons cumin seeds
1 tablespoon medium curry powder
1 tablespoon whole milk natural yogurt
100g fresh white breadcrumbs

1 small handful fresh mint leaves, finely chopped
1 small egg, lightly beaten

To serve
Flatbreads
Raita (see my recipes from page 80)
Lemon wedges

12 metal skewers

1. Place the mince in a bowl and season well with salt and pepper.

2. Add all of the remaining ingredients and, using your fingers, mix thoroughly to combine.

3. Divide the mixture into 12 portions, and mould each one around a metal skewer into a long sausage shape.

4. Place the skewers on a lightly oiled grill rack. Cook under a medium-hot grill for 10-12 minutes, turning halfway through cooking, until cooked through and lightly browned.

5. Serve immediately with warmed flatbreads, raita and lemon wedges.

Kashmiri Lamb Chops

Kashmiri Lamb Chops

Marinating lamb chops is a simple way to pack in plenty of flavour. I prefer them cooked slightly pink, so the meat remains tender and juicy.

Serves 4 10 mins preparation, 10 mins cooking

Ingredients
12 lamb chops or cutlets

For the Kashmiri marinade
1 large pinch saffron strands
2 teaspoons garlic paste
1 teaspoon ginger paste
100g whole milk natural yogurt
1 teaspoon ground cumin
1 teaspoon Kashmiri chilli powder
1 teaspoon ground turmeric

½ teaspoon ground cardamom
Juice of ½ lemon
Sea salt

To serve
Saffron and cardamom pilau
(see page 90 for my recipe)
Salad

1. Soak the saffron strands in 2 tablespoons of boiling water for 3-4 minutes.

2. Meanwhile, place the garlic paste and ginger paste in a bowl with the remaining marinade ingredients. Season well with salt and stir in the saffron mixture.

3. Add the lamb chops to the marinade and toss to coat evenly. Leave to marinate for at least 4-5 minutes.

4. Cook the lamb on a smoking-hot griddle pan, or under a medium-hot grill, for 2-3 minutes on each side, or until cooked to your liking.

5. Serve with saffron and cardamom pilau and salad.

Masala Pork Tikki

Although I've used pork here, you can make these spicy patties with any kind of mince – turkey, chicken, lamb or beef. Whatever you choose, you'll soon realise that one is never enough!

Serves 4 6-8 mins preparation, 20 mins cooking

Ingredients
500g minced pork
6 spring onions, finely chopped
1 teaspoon garlic paste
1 teaspoon ginger paste
1 small bunch fresh coriander (stalks and leaves), finely chopped
2 tablespoons Madras curry paste
50g fresh white breadcrumbs
Vegetable oil for shallow frying

To serve
Chutney or raita (see my recipes from page 80)
Lime wedges

1. In a bowl, mix the mince with the spring onions, garlic paste, ginger paste, chopped coriander, Madras curry paste and breadcrumbs.

2. With wet hands, divide the mixture into 12 portions, and shape each one into a flat cake or patty.

3. In a large, non-stick frying pan heat the oil and shallow-fry the patties in 2 batches. They'll need around 5 minutes on each side, until browned and cooked through.

4. Remove from oil and place on kitchen paper to drain.

5. Serve with your choice of chutney or raita and lime wedges.

Masala Pork Tikki

Fish & Shellfish

The marriage of fresh fish and seafood with the subtle complexity of Indian spices works brilliantly – delicious as well as naturally low in fat. Like all my recipes, these are quick and easy to cook, and very versatile. Try them as main courses, or use smaller quantities to make tasty, nutritious starters.

Patrani Macchi

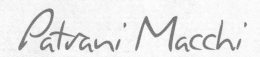

Patrani Macchi

From the western shores of India, this delicious baked fish dish looks very impressive when you serve it wrapped in banana leaves. Let your guests unwrap their individual parcels at the table, releasing mouth-watering aromas. (If you can't get fresh banana leaves, you can use lightly oiled foil or baking parchment instead).

Serves 4 15 mins preparation, 15 mins cooking

Ingredients
4 thick salmon fillets, skinned
2 teaspoons ground turmeric
Fresh banana leaves for wrapping (available from Asian grocers or supermarkets)

For the spice paste
2 teaspoons ground cumin
2 teaspoons ground coriander
1½ teaspoons jaggery or palm sugar
100g coconut cream
100g freshly grated coconut (if you use frozen, make sure it's thawed)
4 fresh red chillies, deseeded and chopped
100g fresh coriander (stalks and leaves), chopped

20g fresh mint leaves, chopped
2 teaspoons garlic paste
1 teaspoon ginger paste
4 tablespoons vegetable oil
Juice of 2 limes
2 teaspoons sea salt

To serve
Basmati rice
Tarka dal (see page 62 for my recipe)
Kachumber (see page 80 for my recipe)
Lemon wedges

Food processor

1. Pre-heat the oven to 200°C/fan 180°C/gas mark 6.

2. Make the spice paste by placing all the paste ingredients in a food processer and blending until fairly smooth.

3. Place the fish fillets on a plate, in a single layer. Sprinkle with turmeric, rubbing it into the fish, and keep to one side.

4. Cut the banana leaves into four 24cm squares, and soften by dipping into a pan of very hot water for a few seconds. Wipe dry with kitchen paper and arrange on a work surface.

5. Spread the spice paste thickly on both sides of each piece of fish.

6. Place a piece of fish on each banana leaf, and wrap it up like a parcel, securing with bamboo skewers or string.

7. Place the parcels on a baking sheet, and bake in the oven for 12-15 minutes until cooked through.

8. Serve immediately with basmati rice, tarka dal, kachumber and lemon wedges.

Meen Moilee

This lightly spiced curry from the coastal region of Kerala is a great example of India's minimalist cooking with maximum flavour. It's all about fresh ingredients, combined in a simple but effective way.

Serves 4 10 mins preparation, 20 mins cooking

Ingredients
2 teaspoons sea salt
2 teaspoons ground turmeric
4 x 200g halibut fillets or steaks
2 tablespoons vegetable oil
2 onions, finely sliced
4 fresh green chillies, slit lengthways
3 garlic cloves, thinly sliced
12 fresh curry leaves

400ml coconut milk
100ml water
1 handful fresh coriander leaves, finely chopped
Juice of 1 lime

To serve
Basmati rice
Poppadoms

1. Mix a teaspoon of salt with a teaspoon of turmeric. Rub this gently into the fish fillets or steaks, and keep to one side.

2. Heat the oil in a large, non-stick saucepan. Add the onion, chillies, garlic and curry leaves, and stir-fry for 6-8 minutes over a medium-low heat, until the onion is translucent.

3. Add the remaining salt and turmeric to the pan. Pour in the coconut milk and water, and bring to the boil.

4. Add the fish to the pan, in a single layer. Reduce the heat to medium and simmer for 6-8 minutes, turning the fish after 3-4 minutes. It should be just cooked through.

5. Remove the pan from the heat, sprinkle with coriander and stir in the lime juice.

6. Serve with basmati rice and poppadoms.

Meen Moilee

Indian-Style Crab Salad

The delicate taste and texture of white crab meat works perfectly when combined with this simple and delicious salad.

Serves 4 15 mins preparation, 5 mins cooking

Ingredients

2 tablespoons vegetable oil
2 garlic cloves, finely chopped
1 teaspoon fresh ginger, grated
1 fresh red chilli, deseeded and finely chopped
6 fresh curry leaves
2 teaspoons cumin seeds
4 spring onions, finely sliced
600g cooked white crab meat

½ cucumber, deseeded and finely chopped
2 plum tomatoes, finely chopped
Juice of 1 lime
1 small handful fresh coriander leaves, chopped
1 small handful fresh mint leaves, chopped
Sea salt and milled black pepper
50g wild rocket leaves

1. Heat the oil in a non-stick frying pan over a high heat. Add the garlic, ginger, chilli, curry leaves and cumin seeds, and stir-fry for 1-2 minutes.

2. Stir in the spring onions and crab meat, and stir-fry for a further 1-2 minutes.

3. Take the pan off the heat and stir in the cucumber, tomatoes, lime juice, coriander and mint. Season with salt and pepper and mix well.

4. Divide the rocket between 4 serving plates and top with the crab mixture.

Indian-Style Crab Salad

Masala Bhangda

Masala Bhangda

One of the most sustainable fish in our waters, mackerel is also cheap, nutritious and full of flavour. Most importantly, it's very easy to cook, as you can see from this quick, tasty recipe.

Serves 4 10 mins preparation, 20 mins cooking

Ingredients

125g whole milk natural yogurt
3 teaspoons garlic paste
1 teaspoon ground cumin
½ teaspoon ground turmeric
1 teaspoon ground coriander
2 tablespoons Kashmiri chilli powder
1 teaspoon sea salt
Juice of 1 lime

8 fresh mackerel fillets
1 small handful fresh coriander leaves, chopped

To serve
Lime wedges
Salad

1. In a large bowl, whisk together the yogurt, garlic paste, cumin, turmeric, ground coriander, chilli powder, salt and lime juice.

2. Make 3-4 diagonal slashes on the skin side of each mackerel fillet. Add the fillets to the yogurt mixture and coat well. Leave to marinate for 5 minutes.

3. Pre-heat the grill to medium-high.

4. Place the mackerel fillets, on a lightly oiled grill rack, in a single layer. Grill for 6-8 minutes, or until lightly browned and cooked through.

5. Sprinkle the fillets with chopped coriander and serve with lime wedges and salad.

Goan Teesri

The secret of this curry's wonderfully complex flavours is the Goan masala – an aromatic blend of spices and herbs that you simply mix together. When added to coconut milk, onion, and the other ingredients, it makes a really distinctive curry that also works well with fresh tiger or king prawns, or mussels.

Serves 4 6-8 mins preparation, 20 mins cooking

Ingredients
3 tablespoons vegetable oil
200g onion, chopped
4 tablespoons tomato purée
400ml coconut milk
100ml water
2 fresh green chillies, slit lengthways
1kg live clams, washed
1 teaspoon mustard seeds
10-12 fresh curry leaves

For the Goan spice masala
¼ teaspoon ground cloves
1 tablespoon ground coriander

1 teaspoon ground cumin
2 tablespoons Kashmiri chilli powder
¼ teaspoon ground star anise
½ teaspoon ground turmeric
1 tablespoon jaggery or palm sugar
3 teaspoons garlic paste
2 teaspoons ginger paste
1½ tablespoons white wine vinegar

To serve
1 handful fresh coriander leaves, chopped
Basmati rice

1. Mix all of the masala ingredients together in a bowl and keep to one side.

2. Heat 2 tablespoons of the oil in a large saucepan over a medium-high heat. Add the onion and stir-fry for 1-2 minutes before stirring in the masala mix. Keep stirring and cook for 2 more minutes, releasing the aromas of the spices. Stir in the tomato purée, and stir-fry for another minute.

3. Stir in the coconut milk and water, add the chillies and bring to the boil.

4. Turn the heat down to medium and cook for about 10 minutes, until the sauce has thickened slightly. Taste for seasoning.

5. Add the clams, cover the pan with a lid and give it a good shake. Cook over a high heat for about 5-6 minutes, until the clams have opened up and are cooked through. Shake the pan occasionally, and discard any clams that remain shut.

6. While the clams are cooking, heat the remaining oil in a frying pan on a high heat, then add the mustard seeds and curry leaves. Cook for 30 seconds until the seeds begin to pop, and then stir into the curry.

7. Garnish with chopped coriander and serve with freshly cooked basmati rice.

Spiced Prawns with Nigella Seeds and Curry Leaves

Spiced Prawns with Nigella Seeds and Curry Leaves

For easy entertaining, this dish is very straightforward and full of flavour. You can even do the preparation in advance, with only a little last-minute stir-frying before you serve.

Serves 4 6-8 mins preparation, 10 mins cooking

Ingredients

600g raw king prawns, peeled
(with the veins removed and tails left on)
1 teaspoon Kashmiri chilli powder
1 fresh green chilli, finely sliced
Sea salt and milled black pepper
3 tablespoons vegetable oil
1-2 teaspoons nigella seeds
1 teaspoon cumin seeds

2 garlic cloves, finely chopped
15 fresh curry leaves
2 tomatoes, finely chopped

To serve
Basmati rice

1. Place the prawns, chilli powder and chilli in a mixing bowl. Season with salt and pepper, and mix well. (If you want to do this stage in advance, you can cover the prawns and keep in the fridge until you need them, for up to 24 hours.)

2. Heat the oil in a wok or large non-stick frying pan, over a medium-high heat. When hot, add the nigella seeds and cumin seeds. As soon as they begin to pop, stir in the garlic.

3. Quickly add the prawns and curry leaves. Stir-fry for 1 minute, then add the chopped tomatoes.

4. Stir-fry for a further 2-3 minutes, then turn the heat down to medium-low. Let the prawns cook gently for 2-3 minutes, stirring until they just turn pink and are cooked through.

5. Serve immediately with freshly cooked basmati rice.

Samudrapheni Masala

The best way to enjoy these irresistible morsels is simply with a glass of chilled beer. Inspired by the cuisine of the Konkan coastline of Western India, they're quick and easy to prepare as a tasty snack or lunch.

Serves 4 10 mins preparation, 12-15 mins cooking

Ingredients
500g prepared squid rings
6 tablespoons fine semolina
6 tablespoons cornflour
1 teaspoon Kashmiri chilli powder
¼ teaspoon ground turmeric
Vegetable oil for deep frying

2 teaspoons garlic paste
2 teaspoons ginger paste
2 tablespoons white wine vinegar
2 teaspoons ground cumin
1 teaspoon ground coriander
1 teaspoon sea salt

For the marinade
2 teaspoons chilli paste
1 teaspoon dried red chilli flakes

To serve
Lime wedges

1. Place all of the marinade ingredients in a mixing bowl, stir well and add the squid. Toss to coat the rings evenly and keep to one side for 5 minutes.

2. In a separate bowl, mix together the semolina, cornflour, chilli powder and turmeric.

3. Half fill a large saucepan with vegetable oil. Place over a high heat until it reaches 180-190°C (or until a cube of bread browns in 25-30 seconds).

4. Remove the squid rings from the marinade, and toss in the semolina mixture, shaking off any excess mixture.

5. Deep-fry the squid rings in batches for 1-2 minutes, or until crisp and golden.

6. Remove from the oil with a slotted spoon, and place on kitchen paper to drain.

7. Serve immediately with lime wedges.

Samudrapheni Masala

Vegetables & Pulses

With its long history of vegetarian cooking, India is a wonderful source of vegetable-based recipes. Try these dishes as a starter to accompany any of the other recipes in this book. Or combine them to create a vegetarian feast. A tasty way to get your 'five a day'!

Tandoori Broccoli

Tandoori Broccoli

Broccoli is a lovely vegetable, but if you're having it with a curry, you need to do more than just boil it. Here you coat it with a creamy, spicy marinade and then just grill it – very simple, but always a favourite. It works well with cauliflower too.

Serves 4 10 mins preparation, 6-8 mins cooking

Ingredients

1 head of broccoli, cut into large florets
150g Greek yogurt
1 tablespoon lemongrass, finely chopped or lemongrass paste
Juice and finely grated zest of 1 lime
50g cream cheese
1 teaspoon green chilli paste

1 teaspoon garlic paste
1 teaspoon ginger paste
1 teaspoon tandoori paste
Sea salt and milled black pepper

8 metal skewers

1. Blanch the broccoli in a pan of boiling, lightly salted water for 1 minute. Drain and rinse under cold running water, then drain again and pat dry with kitchen paper.

2. Place the remaining ingredients in a large mixing bowl, season with salt and pepper, and whisk until smooth.

3. Add the broccoli to this mixture and toss to coat evenly.

4. Pre-heat the grill to medium-high.

5. Thread the broccoli florets onto 8 metal skewers and place under the grill. Cook for 3-4 minutes, turning once, until the coating begins to brown and the broccoli is just cooked, and still firm.

6. Remove from the grill and serve immediately.

Beetroot and Coconut Curry

It's the vibrant colour of this curry that hits you first – and when you taste it, you won't be disappointed. The sweetness of the beetroot works perfectly with the fragrant spices, and the coconut milk softens its natural earthiness.

Serves 4 10 mins preparation, 20 mins cooking

Ingredients

2 tablespoons vegetable oil
¼ teaspoon black mustard seeds
1 onion, chopped
2 garlic cloves, chopped
2 fresh green chillies, deseeded and sliced
2 bay leaves
¼ teaspoon ground turmeric
2 teaspoons cumin seeds
1 cinnamon stick
400g raw beetroot, peeled and
cut into thin matchsticks

2 tomatoes, roughly chopped
250ml water
1 pinch sea salt
200ml coconut milk
Juice of 1 lime

To serve

1 handful fresh coriander leaves, chopped
Basmati rice

1. Heat the oil in a large frying pan and add the mustard seeds. As soon as they begin to pop, add the onion, garlic and chillies, and fry for 1-2 minutes until the onion has softened.

2. Add the bay leaves, turmeric, cumin seeds, cinnamon stick and beetroot, and fry for a further 1-2 minutes.

3. Add the tomatoes, water and a pinch of salt. Leave to simmer for 10 minutes, stirring occasionally, until the beetroot is tender.

4. Stir in the coconut milk, and simmer for another 1-2 minutes until the sauce has thickened.

5. Stir in the lime juice, and check the seasoning, adding more salt if necessary.

6. Garnish with chopped coriander and serve with freshly cooked basmati rice.

Beetroot and Coconut Curry

Tarka Dal

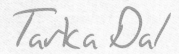

Tarka Dal

The word 'dal' simply means lentils, and there are many regional variations in how to cook them, using different types of lentils. In this recipe I've used red split lentils, as they're easy to find and don't need pre-soaking. 'Tarka' is the way we add the final seasoning to the dish – here it's a spiced oil. You can eat this as a side dish, or make a meal of it with rice and pickles.

Serves 4 6-8 mins preparation, 20 mins cooking

Ingredients
200g red split lentils, washed and drained
1 teaspoon ground turmeric
1 teaspoon ground coriander
1 teaspoon ground cumin
2 fresh green chillies, split lengthways
1 teaspoon ginger paste
2 tomatoes, deseeded and chopped
1 large handful fresh coriander (stalks and leaves), finely chopped
Sea salt

For the tarka
3 tablespoons vegetable oil
1 teaspoon black mustard seeds
2 teaspoons cumin seeds
10 fresh curry leaves
4 garlic cloves, thinly sliced
1 dried red chilli

To serve
Basmati rice
Pickles

1. Place the lentils in a large saucepan. Add 1 litre of boiling water and bring to the boil over a high heat. Skim off any foam that comes to the surface.

2. Turn the heat to medium and add the turmeric, ground coriander, ground cumin, green chillies and ginger paste. Cook for 15-20 minutes, stirring occasionally, until the mixture is thickened and the lentils are tender.

3. Meanwhile, make the tarka by heating the oil in a small, non-stick saucepan over a medium-high heat. When hot, add the mustard seeds, cumin seeds, curry leaves, garlic and dried red chilli.

4. Stir-fry for 1 minute, then take off the heat and stir into the lentil mixture with the tomatoes and chopped coriander.

5. Season with salt, and serve immediately with basmati rice and any pickles you like.

Bhindi Masala

Bhindi Masala

If you've never tried okra before, this is a great way to enjoy it. The spices and garlic really bring out its sweetness, and when it's cooked quickly like this, the texture is just right – soft yet still with a little bite.

Serves 4 10 mins preparation, 10-15 mins cooking

Ingredients

4 tablespoons vegetable oil
1 teaspoon black mustard seeds
2 teaspoons cumin seeds
2 onions, halved and sliced
2 teaspoons garlic paste
2 teaspoons ginger paste
2 fresh green chillies, finely sliced
1 teaspoon ground coriander

400g okra, trimmed and cut diagonally into 1cm slices
2 tomatoes, roughly chopped
Sea salt

To serve
Rotis (see page 96 for my recipe)
Pickle or chutney

1. Heat the oil in a non-stick frying pan over a high heat and add the black mustard seeds. When they start to pop, add the cumin seeds, onion, garlic paste, ginger paste, chillies and ground coriander. Stir-fry for 1-2 minutes

2. Add the okra and stir-fry for another 3-4 minutes.

3. Stir in the tomatoes, season with salt and continue to stir-fry over a high heat for a further 4-5 minutes or until the okra is just tender.

4. Remove from the heat and serve immediately with freshly cooked rotis, and pickle or chutney.

Upma

In Southern India, this is a very popular savoury breakfast dish. Try it as a spicy addition to a Sunday brunch, or for a light lunch or supper.

Serves 4 10 mins preparation, 20 mins cooking

Ingredients

175g coarse semolina
2 tablespoons vegetable oil
2 tablespoons butter
1 teaspoon black mustard seeds
1 teaspoon cumin seeds
1 dried red chilli
10-12 fresh curry leaves
1 red onion, chopped

2 tablespoons cashew nuts, roasted
50g frozen peas
600ml boiling vegetable stock
Sea salt and milled black pepper
Juice of ½ lemon
2 tablespoons fresh coconut, grated
1 small handful fresh coriander leaves, chopped
1 tomato, finely chopped

1. Heat a large non-stick frying pan over a medium heat and add the semolina. Dry-fry for 1-2 minutes, then transfer to a bowl or plate and keep to one side.

2. Add the oil and butter to the frying pan and place over a high heat. Add the mustard seeds, cumin seeds, dried chilli and curry leaves. When the mustard seeds start to pop, add the onion and stir-fry for 1-2 minutes.

3. Add the cashew nuts, peas, semolina and stock. Season well with salt and pepper and cook over a gentle heat, stirring constantly until all the liquid has been absorbed. This should take around 10-12 minutes.

4. Remove the pan from the heat and stir in the lemon juice. Garnish with the coconut, coriander and tomato before serving.

Khumbi Korma

Khumbi Korma

For vegetarian entertaining, this Northern Indian mushroom curry is sure to impress. The cashew nuts give it a satisfying texture, and its mild spiciness suits most tastes.

Serves 4 10 mins preparation, 15 mins cooking

Ingredients

2 tablespoons vegetable oil
1 onion, chopped
1 teaspoon garlic paste
1 teaspoon ginger paste
500g mixed open and closed cup mushrooms, roughly chopped or sliced
100g frozen peas
100g cashew nuts, roasted
4 tablespoons korma curry paste

400ml coconut milk
1 squeeze lemon juice
1 pinch sugar
Sea salt

To serve

Saffron and cardamom pilau
(see page 90 for my recipe)

1. Heat the oil in a frying pan. Add the onion and sauté over a medium heat for 2-3 minutes.

2. Add the garlic paste, ginger paste and mushrooms, and sauté for a further 5-6 minutes, or until the mushrooms are lightly browned.

3. Stir in the peas, cashew nuts, korma paste, coconut milk, lemon juice and sugar. Bring to the boil, then simmer uncovered for 5-6 minutes, or until the sauce has thickened slightly.

4. Season with salt to taste, and serve with saffron and cardamom pilau.

Bund Ghobi Bhaji

Bund Ghobi Bhaji

Crisp, tender cabbage, enlivened with the spices and flavours of Southern India, makes an appetising accompaniment to a curry with rice and pickles.

Serves 4 10 mins preparation, 10 mins cooking

Ingredients

3 tablespoons vegetable oil
1 teaspoon mustard seeds
1 teaspoon nigella seeds
1 teaspoon cumin seeds
2 dried red chillies, whole
1½ teaspoons ginger, finely chopped
10-12 fresh curry leaves

1 medium white cabbage, halved, cored and finely shredded
½ teaspoon ground turmeric
50g peanuts, roasted and roughly chopped
50g fresh coconut, grated
Juice of ½ lime
Sea salt and milled black pepper

1. Heat the oil in a large, non-stick frying pan. Add the mustard seeds, nigella seeds and cumin seeds, and stir-fry for 20-30 seconds.

2. Add the red chillies, ginger and curry leaves, and stir-fry for a further 10 seconds.

3. Add the cabbage and turmeric, and stir-fry for 6-8 minutes more, until the cabbage is lightly browned and just tender, but still slightly crisp.

4. Stir in the peanuts, coconut and lime juice. Season well with salt and pepper and serve immediately.

Chole Palak

Chole Palak

In this healthy, protein-rich dish, chickpeas are cooked with spinach, tomatoes and spices. It's as tasty as it is wholesome – I love it with warmed Indian breads.

Serves 4 6-8 mins preparation, 20 mins cooking

Ingredients

4 tablespoons vegetable oil
2 teaspoons cumin seeds
2 onions, chopped
1 teaspoon garlic paste
1 teaspoon ginger paste
1 fresh green chilli, deseeded and thinly sliced
1½ teaspoons dried mango powder (amchoor)
1 teaspoon jaggery or palm sugar
1½ teaspoons garam masala
½ teaspoon ground turmeric

1 teaspoon Kashmiri chilli powder
500g carton passata with onion and garlic
800g tinned chickpeas, drained
200g baby spinach leaves
Sea salt

To serve
Warmed Indian breads or naan

1. Heat the oil in a large, non-stick frying pan over a medium-high heat. Add the cumin seeds and stir-fry for 20-30 seconds, then add the onion, garlic paste, ginger paste and green chilli, and stir-fry for 3-4 minutes.

2. Stir in the mango powder, jaggery or palm sugar, garam masala, ground tumeric, chilli powder and passata. Cook over a high heat for 6-8 minutes, stirring regularly, adding a little water if it gets too thick.

3. Stir in the chickpeas and spinach and cook for 3-4 minutes, or until the spinach has wilted.

4. Season well with salt and serve immediately with warmed Indian breads or naan.

Rajma

Rajma

Wholesome, warming and high in fibre, this Northern Indian dish provides a substantial, flavoursome meal for vegetarians and meat lovers alike. I usually serve it with warmed flatbread and a simple salad.

Serves 4 10 mins preparation, 20 mins cooking

Ingredients
2 tablespoons vegetable oil
2 teaspoons cumin seeds
1 onion, finely chopped
3 teaspoons garlic paste
2 teaspoons ginger paste
2 fresh green chillies, finely chopped
2 large tomatoes, roughly chopped
2 teaspoons ground coriander
1 teaspoon ground cumin
¼ teaspoon ground turmeric
1 teaspoon garam masala

2 x 400g tinned red kidney beans, drained and rinsed
1 teaspoon jaggery or palm sugar
300ml warm water
100ml double cream
Sea salt

To serve
Warmed flatbread
Simple salad
1 handful fresh coriander leaves, finely chopped

1. Heat the oil in a deep pan and add the cumin seeds. When they stop sizzling, add the onion, garlic paste, ginger paste, chillies, tomatoes, ground coriander, cumin, turmeric and garam masala, and stir-fry over a medium heat for 3-4 minutes.

2. Add the kidney beans, jaggery or palm sugar, warm water and cream. Season well with salt and cook over a high heat for 10-12 minutes, stirring often, until the curry thickens.

3. Take off the heat, serve with warmed flatbread, a simple salad and garnish with the chopped coriander.

Mumbai Aloo

These spiced potatoes are really easy to make and go with almost anything! If you have any leftovers, try them wrapped in a chapati or roti for a quick lunch or snack.

Serves 4 10 mins preparation, 20 mins cooking

Ingredients

500g medium potatoes, peeled and diced
4 tablespoons sunflower oil
1-2 teaspoons black mustard seeds
1 teaspoon Kashmiri chilli powder
4 teaspoons cumin seeds
2 teaspoons sesame seeds
8-10 fresh curry leaves
2 teaspoons ground cumin
2 teaspoons ground coriander

1 teaspoon ground turmeric
Sea salt and milled black pepper
1 large handful fresh coriander leaves, chopped
4 tablespoons pomegranate seeds
1 squeeze lemon juice

To serve
Flatbread

1. Boil the potatoes in a large saucepan of lightly salted water for 6-8 minutes, or until just tender. Drain and keep to one side.

2. Heat the oil in a large, non-stick wok or frying pan over a medium-high heat. Add the mustard seeds, chilli powder, cumin seeds, sesame seeds and curry leaves, and stir-fry for 20-30 seconds.

3. Add the ground cumin, ground coriander, ground tumeric and the boiled potatoes. Season well with salt and pepper, and stir-fry briskly over a high heat for 4-5 minutes.

4. Remove from the heat, and stir in the chopped coriander and pomegranate seeds. Squeeze the lemon juice over, and serve while hot with flatbread.

Mumbai Aloo

Sides

Cooling raita, crunchy salads and creamy chutney. Made well, they can turn an Indian meal into a banquet. For special occasions, I like to make two or three side dishes, so people can mix and match. And all these recipes are so quick to prepare, you can do the same in very little time.

Kachumber

You can serve Kachumber as a side salad with almost any Indian meal. Its zesty, spicy flavours are especially good with grilled fish or meat.

Serves 4 10 mins preparation

Ingredients
1 red onion, finely chopped
4 ripe tomatoes, deseeded and finely chopped
1 cucumber, finely chopped
1 fresh green chilli, deseeded and finely chopped
1 small handful fresh coriander leaves,
finely chopped

Juice of 2 large limes
Sea salt and milled black pepper
1 tablespoon peanuts, roasted and roughly
chopped (optional)

1. Put the onion, tomatoes, cucumber, chilli and coriander into a bowl, and pour the lime juice over.

2. Season well with salt and pepper, cover and leave to stand at room temperature for 10-15 minutes.

3. Before serving, mix well and sprinkle with peanuts, if you're using them.

Coriander and Coconut Chutney

Try this fresh, tangy chutney with virtually any main course or starter – its fragrant creaminess works well with most other savoury flavours.

Serves 4 10 mins preparation

Ingredients
100g fresh coconut, finely grated (if you use
frozen, make sure it's thawed)
1 fresh green chilli, chopped
50g fresh coriander (stalks and leaves), chopped
25g fresh mint leaves, chopped
1 teaspoon garlic paste

1 teaspoon ginger paste
100ml natural whole milk yogurt
Juice of 2 limes
Sea salt and milled black pepper

Small food processor

1. Place all the ingredients (except the salt and pepper) in a small food processor and blend until fairly smooth. If it's very thick, add a little extra yogurt.

2. Season the chutney well with salt and pepper, and chill in the fridge until you're ready to serve.

Kachumber & Coriander and Coconut Chutney

Bhindi Ki Raita

Bhindi Ki Raita

Raita's job is to cool things down when you're eating a spicy dish – but it should have interesting flavours of its own. This one, from the Western shores of India, is slightly sweet and gently spiced, and the crisp okra gives it a satisfying texture.

Serves 4   10 mins preparation, 5 mins cooking

Ingredients

6 tablespoons vegetable oil
200g fresh okra, trimmed and cut into thick slices
400ml natural whole milk yogurt
1 teaspoon caster sugar
1 teaspoon cayenne pepper
¼ teaspoon ground turmeric

1 teaspoon ground cumin
Sea salt and milled black pepper
1 teaspoon black mustard seeds
1 small handful fresh coriander leaves, finely chopped

1. Heat 5 tablespoons of the oil in a large frying pan over a medium heat. When it's very hot, add the okra and toss in the oil. Let it sizzle and cook for 3-4 minutes, stirring occasionally. It will slowly turn crisp and brown.

2. Once the okra is well browned, place on kitchen paper to drain and keep to one side until you're ready to serve.

3. Whisk the yogurt and sugar in a medium serving dish. Sprinkle the cayenne pepper, turmeric and cumin over the top, and season well with salt and pepper.

4. Heat the remaining oil in a small frying pan over a high heat. When it begins to smoke, add the mustard seeds. When they've stopped popping, pour the hot oil directly on top of the cayenne pepper, turmeric and cumin (this cooks the powdered spices without burning them).

5. Place the crisp okra on top and serve garnished with coriander.

Gujarati-Style Grated Carrot Salad

Gujarati – Style Grated Carrot Salad

Fresh, crunchy and wholesome, this quick salad gives you lots of tastes and textures for very little effort.

Serves 4 10 mins preparation, 2 mins cooking

Ingredients

2 large carrots, peeled and coarsely grated or shredded
¼ small red cabbage, finely shredded
½ red onion, halved and thinly sliced
4 tablespoons vegetable oil
2 teaspoons black mustard seeds
1 teaspoon caster sugar
1 garlic clove, crushed

½ teaspoon ground cumin
½ teaspoon crushed chilli flakes
Juice of ½ orange
Juice of 1 lemon
Sea salt and milled black pepper
1 small handful fresh coriander leaves, chopped
1 small handful fresh mint leaves, chopped

1. Place the carrots, cabbage and onion into a salad bowl.

2. Heat the oil in a small frying pan. When hot, add the mustard seeds and cook until they start to pop.

3. Pour the oil and mustard seeds over the grated carrot mixture, along with the sugar, garlic, cumin, chilli flakes, and orange and lemon juice.

4. Season the salad well with salt and pepper and toss to mix thoroughly. Then cover and chill in the fridge until you're ready to serve.

5. Just before serving, scatter the salad with coriander and mint, and toss again.

Lobia Salad

Serves 4 10 mins preparation, 10 mins cooking

Ingredients

2 medium potatoes, peeled and diced

100g green beans, cut into 2cm pieces

400g tinned black-eyed beans, drained and rinsed

4 spring onions, thinly sliced

1 fresh red chilli, deseeded and thinly sliced

2 plum tomatoes, deseeded and finely chopped

1 small handful fresh coriander leaves, chopped

1 small handful fresh mint leaves, chopped

For the dressing

2 tablespoons light olive oil

Juice of 1 lemon

1 teaspoon chilli powder

1 teaspoon runny honey

Sea salt and milled black pepper

1. Cook the potatoes in a saucepan of lightly salted boiling water for 8-10 minutes, or until just tender, adding the green beans for the last 2 minutes of cooking time.

2. Drain the potatoes and green beans, and place in a serving bowl with the black-eyed beans, spring onions, chilli, tomatoes, coriander and mint.

3. Mix all the dressing ingredients together, seasoning well with salt and pepper.

4. Stir the dressing into the salad, and mix thoroughly. Serve immediately.

Cucumber, Mint and Pomegranate Raita

Serves 4 6-8 mins preparation, 1 min cooking

Ingredients

1 cucumber, coarsely grated

250ml natural whole milk yogurt, whisked

2 tablespoons vegetable oil

1 teaspoon black mustard seeds

4 fresh curry leaves

2 whole dried red chillies, broken in half

2 teaspoons cumin seeds

4 tablespoons fresh coconut, grated

1 small handful fresh coriander leaves, finely chopped

Sea salt and milled black pepper

2 tablespoons pomegranate seeds

2 tablespoons peanuts, roasted and roughly chopped

1. Place the cucumber in a bowl with the yogurt.

2. Heat the oil in a frying pan, and add the mustard seeds, curry leaves, chillies and cumin seeds. Stir-fry for 1 minute, then remove from the heat and stir into the cucumber mixture along with the coconut and coriander.

3. Season well with salt and pepper. Mix and transfer the raita to a serving dish. Scatter over the pomegranate seeds and peanuts, and chill in the fridge until you're ready to serve.

Lobia Salad & Cucumber, Mint and Pomegranate Raita

Rice & Breads

No Indian meal is complete without rice or
bread. Simple boiled or steamed rice is the
most popular, but it's nice to try something
different with some more interesting recipes,
like my saffron and cardamom pilau.
Or try my puris and rotis – two classic
Indian breads.

Saffron and Cardamom Pilau

Saffron and Cardamom Pilau

Saffron is quite an expensive ingredient, but just a pinch is all you need to add a wonderful, luxurious flavour to this aromatic rice dish.

Serves 4 5 mins preparation, 8-10 mins cooking, 5-6 mins resting

Ingredients

275g basmati rice
3 tablespoons ghee (Indian clarified butter)
1 cinnamon stick
6-8 green cardamom pods
10 black peppercorns
1 dried bay leaf
3 cloves

1 teaspoon ground turmeric
1 teaspoon saffron strands
600ml boiling vegetable or chicken stock
Sea salt
300ml vegetable oil
1 onion, halved and finely sliced

1. Place the rice in a sieve and rinse under cold running water. Drain thoroughly and keep to one side.

2. Heat the ghee in a heavy based saucepan over a medium heat. Add the cinnamon stick, cardamom pods, peppercorns, bay leaf and cloves and stir-fry for 1-2 minutes. Then add the rice, turmeric, saffron and stock.

3. Season well with salt and bring to the boil. Stir the rice and cover the pan tightly. If the lid isn't very tight, cover the pan with kitchen foil before putting the lid on.

4. Reduce the heat to low and cook for 8-10 minutes.

5. Heat the vegetable oil in a small saucepan over a medium-high heat, add the onion and cook for 1-2 mins until golden brown.

6. Take the rice off the heat and leave to rest, still covered, for 5-6 minutes.

7. When you're ready to serve, uncover the pan and fluff up the rice with a fork.

8. Serve immediately with the onion sprinkled on top.

Jeera and Mutter Pulao

This fragrant rice dish is one of the most versatile – and the perfect accompaniment to a whole range of Indian recipes. For authentic flavour and texture, it's important to use basmati rice, rather than any other long-grain variety.

Serves 4   5 mins preparation, 8-10 mins cooking, 5-6 mins resting

Ingredients

275g basmati rice
3 tablespoons ghee (Indian clarified butter)
10-12 fresh curry leaves
2 teaspoons cumin seeds
1 dried red chilli

1 cinnamon stick
50g cashew nuts, roasted
200g fresh or frozen peas
600ml boiling vegetable or chicken stock
Sea salt

1. Place the rice in a sieve and rinse under cold running water. Drain thoroughly and keep to one side.

2. Heat the ghee in a heavy based saucepan over a medium heat. Add the curry leaves, cumin seeds, chilli, cinnamon stick and cashew nuts. Stir-fry for 1-2 minutes, then add the rice, peas and stock.

3. Season well with salt and bring to the boil. Stir the rice and cover the pan tightly. If the lid isn't very tight, cover the pan with kitchen foil before putting the lid on.

4. Reduce the heat to low and cook for 8-10 minutes.

5. Take the rice off the heat and leave to rest, still covered, for 5-6 minutes.

6. When you're ready to serve, uncover the pan and fluff up the rice with a fork. Serve immediately.

Jeera and Mutter Pulao

Vegetable Pulao

You can enjoy this one-pot vegetable rice dish with any curry – it's delicious with all kinds of spicy dishes. But it's also really good as a meal in itself, with a big dollop of yogurt and perhaps some poppadoms and pickles.

Serves 4 10-12 mins preparation, 8-10 mins cooking, 5-6 mins resting

Ingredients
275g basmati rice
2 tablespoons vegetable oil
2 tablespoons ghee (Indian clarified butter)
50g ready cooked crispy fried onions
1 cinnamon stick
4 green cardamom pods
3 cloves
2 teaspoons cumin seeds

1 teaspoon garlic paste
200g washed baby spinach leaves, roughly chopped
1 tomato, deseeded and roughly chopped
1 large handful fresh dill, finely chopped
Sea salt and milled black pepper
600ml boiling water

1. Place the rice in a sieve and rinse under cold running water. Drain thoroughly and keep to one side.

2. Heat the oil and ghee in a heavy based saucepan over a medium heat. Add the crispy onions, cinnamon stick, cardamom pods, cloves, cumin, garlic paste, spinach and tomato. Stir-fry for 1-2 minutes and then add the rice and dill.

3. Season well with salt and pepper and add the boiling water. Bring to the boil, then stir the rice and cover the pan tightly. If the lid isn't very tight, cover the pan with kitchen foil before putting the lid on.

4. Reduce the heat to low and cook for 8-10 minutes.

5. Take the pan off the heat and leave to rest, still covered, for 5-6 minutes.

6. When you're ready to serve, uncover the pan and fluff up the rice with a fork. Serve immediately.

Vegetable Pulao

Rotis

These basic wholemeal flatbreads (also known as chapatis) are great to eat with Indian meals. You can find chapati flour (sometimes called 'atta') in most large supermarkets and Asian grocers. If you want to make your rotis in advance, you can wrap them in foil and re-heat them in an oven – but they always taste best freshly cooked from the pan.

Makes 8 10 mins preparation, 20 mins cooking

Ingredients
250g chapati flour (atta), plus extra for dusting the work surface
1 teaspoon sea salt
4 tablespoons vegetable oil
170ml warm water

1. Place the flour in a mixing bowl with the salt. Drizzle the oil over the flour mixture and add the warm water. Knead in the bowl until the dough is smooth and elastic.

2. Turn the dough out onto a lightly floured surface and knead for another minute or two.

3. Divide the dough into 8 portions and roll each one into a smooth ball.

4. Roll out each ball to make a thin disc, approximately 20cm in diameter. If the dough begins to stick, sprinkle on some more flour.

5. Place a large, non-stick frying pan over a medium-high heat. When hot, cook the first roti for 2-3 minutes, flipping halfway through cooking and pressing it down with a spatula to cook evenly. It will get lightly browned in places and should look dry.

6. Transfer the roti to a plate, cover with foil and a clean tea towel to keep warm while you make the rest. Serve immediately.

Rotis

Puris

Puris

For a change from chapatis, try these deep-fried, puffy wholemeal breads. I think they're particularly good with spicy potatoes or seafood curries – but be sure to eat them as soon as you've cooked them, because they 'deflate' very quickly!

Makes 12 20 mins preparation, 10 mins cooking

Ingredients
200g chapati flour (atta), plus extra for dusting the work surface
1 teaspoon sea salt
2½ tablespoons vegetable oil
150ml warm water
Vegetable or sunflower oil for deep-frying

Food thermometer

1. Place the flour and salt into a mixing bowl. Make a well in the centre, pour in 2 tablespoons of the oil and work it into the flour mixture with your fingertips.

2. Gradually add the warm water to the flour (a few tablespoons at a time) and continue working with your fingers to form a firm, yet slightly wet and sticky, dough.

3. Knead the dough in the bowl for 3-4 minutes, until it's smooth and no longer sticky. Drizzle the remaining ½ tablespoon of oil over it, and knead again for 1 minute until smooth.

4. Divide the dough into 12 portions and roll each one into a small ball.

5. On a lightly floured surface, use a rolling pin to flatten each ball and roll into an even 12cm disc, to the thickness of a 10p coin. If it sticks while you're doing this, sprinkle on a little extra flour.

6. Fill a deep saucepan or wok with the frying oil (about 5cm deep) and heat over a medium-high heat to 190°C. (Use a cooking thermometer to make sure you don't overheat the oil.)

7. Using a flat, metal slotted spoon, lower one of the dough discs into the oil, pushing it gently under the surface with the back of the spoon to submerge it completely. The puri will begin to puff up – now cook for about 10 seconds, then carefully turn it over and cook for another 8-10 seconds.

8. Remove the puri from the oil with the slotted spoon, and place on kitchen paper to drain while you cook the rest of them, one by one, making sure the temperature stays at 190°C (increasing or decreasing the heat as required).

9. Serve the puris immediately.

Desserts & Drinks

When eating an Indian meal, many people don't save room for dessert – but try the recipes here and you'll see it's well worth it. Full of Eastern flavour and texture, their creaminess is balanced by fruit and nuts. To wash them down, I've included two aromatic teas and two refreshingly fruity cold drinks.

Mango and Cardamom Kulfi

Mango and Cardamom Kulfi

Unlike conventional ice cream, Kulfi doesn't need churning; you simply freeze it in moulds. So it's quick to prepare – and in this recipe, mango purée and cardamom give it a distinctive, refreshing flavour.

Serves 4 10 mins preparation, 6-8 hours freezing

Ingredients
200ml sweetened condensed milk
250ml double cream
150ml tinned Alphonso or Kesar mango purée
1 teaspoon cardamom seeds, finely crushed
2 tablespoons pistachio nuts, finely chopped
2 tablespoons edible rose petals

Electric whisk
4 dariole moulds

1. Place the condensed milk, cream, mango purée and cardamom in a mixing bowl. Using an electric whisk, beat the mixture until it thickens.

2. Spoon the mixture into 4 individual dariole moulds. Cover with foil and cling film, and freeze for 6-8 hours or overnight.

3. When you're ready to serve, dip the moulds in hot water for a few seconds, use a palette knife to loosen the desserts, and turn them out onto serving plates. Sprinkle with the pistachios and edible rose petals, and serve immediately.

Malai Khumani

Originating from the royal state of Hyderabad in Southern India, this creamy, wholesome and slightly exotic dessert is quick to prepare and the perfect ending to a spicy meal.

Serves 4 20 mins preparation, 3-4 hours chilling

Ingredients

200g dried, ready-to-eat apricots
100g golden sultanas
100ml orange juice
300ml double cream
4 tablespoons golden caster sugar

1 teaspoon rose water
4 tablespoons pistachio nuts, finely chopped
4 tablespoons walnuts, finely chopped
4 tablespoons hazelnuts, finely chopped
Edible gold leaf (optional)

1. Roughly chop the apricots and place in a bowl with the sultanas and orange juice. Cover the bowl and keep to one side for 15-20 minutes.

2. In a separate bowl, whisk the cream, sugar and rose water until the mixture forms soft peaks, and fold in the chopped nuts.

3. Divide the apricot mixture between 4 dessert pots or glasses. Spoon over the cream mixture and chill in the fridge for 3-4 hours.

4. These desserts are lovely as they are – or for a special occasion, garnish each one with edible gold leaf and serve immediately.

Malai Khumani

Limbu Pani & Banana and Cardamom Lassi

Limbu Pani

On a warm day, this refreshing drink really revives you – which is why it's so popular all over India. If you prefer, you can use three large lemons instead of the limes.

Serves 4 10 mins preparation

Ingredients
5 large limes
50g caster sugar
250ml cold water
1 pinch sea salt (optional)
350ml chilled soda water

¼ cucumber, sliced
A few sprigs of fresh mint

Food processor

1. Cut one of the limes into chunks and place into a food processor, along with any juice from the chopping board and the juice of the remaining limes. Add the sugar, salt (if you're using it) and a little of the cold water. Whizz to a purée and then add the rest of the cold water. Taste and add a little more sugar if necessary.

2. Pour the drink into a jug and top up with chilled soda water. Add the slices of cucumber and a couple of sprigs of mint, then chill in the fridge until you're ready to serve.

3. Serve over ice with a slice of cucumber and a fresh sprig of mint in each glass.

Banana and Cardamom Lassi

A lassi is a chilled yogurt drink, often flavoured with fruit such as mangoes or strawberries. Here, the marriage of banana and fragrant cardamom is a winner.

Serves 4 6-8 mins preparation

Ingredients
500g whole milk natural yogurt
1-2 tablespoons caster sugar (depending on how sweet you like it)
2 bananas, peeled and roughly chopped

200ml ice cold water
½ teaspoon cardamom seeds, finely crushed

Food processor

1. Place all the ingredients in a food processor and blend for a few minutes until frothy and smooth.

2. Pour the lassi into 4 chilled glasses and serve immediately.

Masala Chai

This sweet, spiced milky tea is an everyday drink for thousands of office workers all over India, where vendors sell it freshly brewed on street corners and train platforms.

Serves 4 5 mins preparation, 7 mins cooking

Ingredients
500ml water
200ml milk
50g caster sugar
2 cinnamon sticks

6 cloves
6 green cardamom pods, lightly crushed
2 slices ginger
1-2 tablespoons Assam loose-leaf tea

1. Pour the water and milk into a saucepan with the sugar, cinnamon sticks, cloves, cardamom pods and ginger. Bring to the boil, reduce the heat to low, and simmer for 5-6 minutes.

2. Put the tea leaves in a teapot and pour in the spiced mixture. Allow to infuse for 4-5 minutes, then using a strainer, pour into teacups.

Lemongrass and Ginger Tea

I love the delicate floral aroma of this drink. It's the perfect afternoon pick-me-up and very soothing after dinner as an alternative to coffee.

Serves 4 5 mins preparation, 6-8 mins cooking

Ingredients
4 stalks lemongrass, plus extra to garnish
1 small knob of ginger, thinly sliced
600ml water
1 green tea bag

To serve
Honey

1. Cut the lemongrass into 4cm lengths and crush with the flat side of a large knife. Place in a saucepan with the ginger and water.

2. Bring to the boil and add the green tea bag. Take the pan off the heat and allow the tea to infuse for 3-4 minutes.

3. Using a fine sieve or strainer, pour the tea into heatproof glasses or cups.

4. Garnish with stalks of lemongrass and serve with honey to sweeten.

Masala Chai & Lemongrass and Ginger Tea

About Howdens Joinery

Anyone who loves to cook will love the Indian kitchen. Combining subtle design influences with a practical approach to versatility and durability, this is the perfect place for cooking, eating and relaxing.

Howdens Joinery offers a range of integrated kitchen, appliance and joinery products designed to meet the needs of modern living.

Our offer includes over 45 different kitchen designs, plus a full range of accessories, worktops, doors, flooring, skirting, and a wide variety of Lamona appliances, sinks and taps, exclusive to Howdens. The Lamona range has been selected to perfectly complement our range of kitchens, and products are manufactured to the highest standards to ensure they are durable and reliable.

Last year we supplied over 350,000 kitchens, 600,000 appliances and 550,000 sinks and taps to UK homes.

To find out more or locate one of over 565 nationwide depots, visit **www.howdens.com**

Bespoke Shelving Unit

Pan Drawer with Internal Storage Drawer

Lamona Professional 5 Burner Gas Hob with
Lamona Stainless Steel Chimney Extractor

Lamona Windermere 1.5 Bowl Sink with Lamona Brushed Steel Effect Garda Swan Neck Monobloc Tap

Burford 4 Panel Oak Glazed Door

About the author

Food stylist and author Sunil Vijayakar developed his love of food while growing up in Bombay – especially with the encouragement of his father, who would take him to the bustling local markets on Sunday mornings. After choosing from aisles of fresh fruit and vegetables, courtyards of fish and shellfish, and pyramids of spices, herbs, nuts and dried fruit, they would head home to prepare a feast for friends and family.

These colourful memories still inspire Sunil's cooking today. Over the past 15 years, he has written more than 40 books such as, "Fresh Indian" and "200 Curries", as well as regularly contributing to magazines. This latest collaboration demonstrates the wonderful wealth of flavours the country has to offer.

www.sunilvijayakar.com

Exclusive to Howdens Joinery Co.

www.lamona.co.uk